The Little Book of Red Flags

A curated anthology of social media musings

Collated by Karen Martin
Illustrations by Thomas Corboy

Copyright © 2024 KazJoyPress

The Moral Rights of the illustrator **Thomas Corboy** have been asserted.

All rights reserved. No part of this book may be reproduced or used in any manner without written permission except for the use of quotations for a book review.

For more information email kazjoypress@gmail.com

First published in Australia in August 2024 by KazJoyPress (Australia) **www.kazjoypress.com**

Book formatting & co-design by Working Type Studio

SEL031000 SELF-HELP / Personal Growth / General
ISBN: 978-0-6451922-4-7 (Paperback)
ISBN 978-0-6451922-8-5 (Hardcover)

A catalogue record for this book is available from the National Library of Australia

Introduction

A *red flag* is a warning sign. In sport it will stop the game because of a foul or danger. In relationships, red flags are not so literal. They are metaphoric signals advising caution. But here's the thing, they are not always obvious. You must be paying attention. Unfortunately, I was distracted.

The Little Book of Red Flags is a tangled dance of love and loss sprinkled with a dash of social media wisdom and a pinch of self-respect. Did I predict the demise of my marriage? Not exactly, although I remember the day when I tearfully confessed to my daughter, 'I think my marriage is over.' I soon discovered this was the opening line of a drama rivalling the worst soap opera imaginable - death by a thousand tears.

Spiraling into crisis, I clung to the belief we could work through the storm. But it needed both of us working together and that ship had sailed. Instead, we played a twisted game of emotional limbo: how low could we go before calling it quits?

Amid the turmoil, I found an anchor: self-respect. It became my lifeline. I ignored the prophetic scrawl in my journal asking *will self-respect kill my marriage.*

Enlightenment shone via screenshots from Instagram. Little digital treasures captured moments of clarity in my ocean of pain. Quotes and musings spoke to my experience. It was only later I recognized their significance.

The Little Book of Red Flags is a curated anthology of social media musings marking my journey toward self-discovery. I have acknowledged authors where possible, but many are sentiments without attribution, and like much on social media platforms, are anonymous. I sought permission from publishers and where possible, utilised work accessible under a Creative Commons license.

So, to you, my dear fellow travelers hiking the tumultuous terrain of relationships, take heed of the signs that appear on your trail, for they speak volumes in 280 characters or less. And as you navigate the prickly path of love and heartache, take care. Pack yourself a bag of self-respect, self-compassion and humour, because it can be brutal out there.

love Karen xx

Having a weird mum builds character

Accountability feels like an attack when you're not ready to acknowledge how your behaviour harms others. Read it again.

I would rather adjust my life to your absence than adjust my boundaries to accommodate your disrespect.

False positivism is when you pretend things aren't really so bad when in fact they are. The most positive thing is always to tell the truth, and sometimes that means shedding light on something that's negative.

@mariannewilliamson

I just got some juice out of the fridge and I swear I heard the wine say 'what the fuck'!

@someecards

Due to personal reasons, I will be going completely off the fucking rails

A Medicine Woman's Prayer

I will not rescue you
For you are not powerless.
I will not fix you.
For you are not broken.
I will not heal you.
For I see you, in your wholeness.
I will walk with you through the darkness
As you remember the light.

@shereeblisstilsley

From time to time you may become restless, and the restlessness will not go away. At such times, just sit quietly, follow your breathing, smile a half-smile, and shine your awareness on the restlessness. Don't judge it or try to destroy it, because this restlessness is you yourself. It is born, has some period of existence, and fades away, quite naturally. Don't be in too big a hurry to find its source. Don't try too hard to make it disappear. Just illuminate it. You will see that little by little it will change, merge, become connected with you, the observer. Any psychological state that you subject to this illumination will eventually soften and acquire the same nature as the observing mind.

Thich Nhat Hanh

When you're not used to being confident, confidence feels like arrogance.
When you're used to being passive, assertiveness feels like aggression.

When you're not used to getting your needs met, prioritizing yourself feels selfish.

Your comfort zone is not a good benchmark.

Dr Vassilia @JunoCounselling

Grief, I've learned, is really just love. It's all the love you want to give, but cannot. All that unspent love gathers up in the corners of your eyes, the lump in your throat, and in that hollow part of your chest. Grief is just love with no place to go.

Jamie Anderson

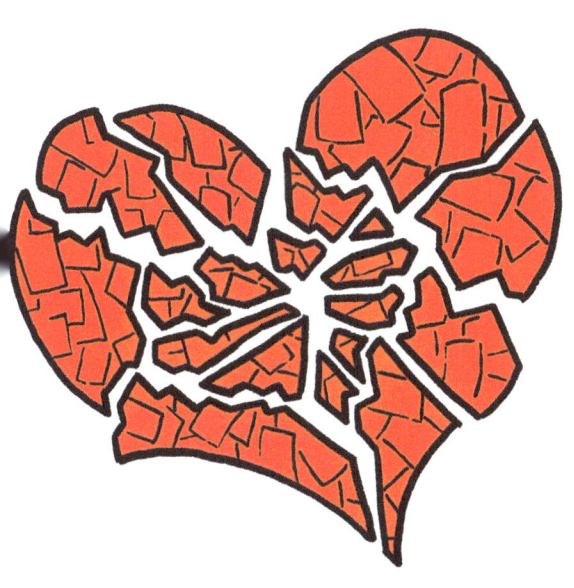

Stop trying to be liked by everybody. You don't even like everybody.

You did not wake up today to be mediocre.

It's National Red Wine Day

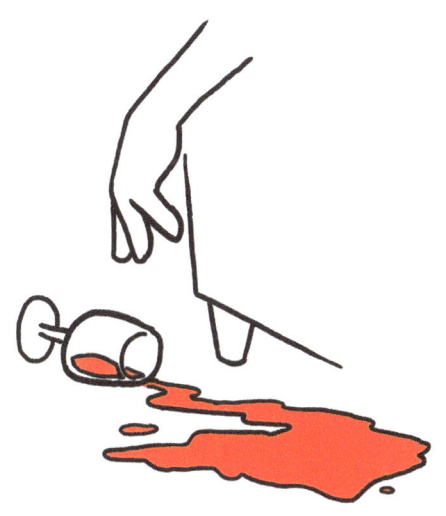

Emotion allows the unconscious access to implant or inject ideas, desires, fears and compulsions, or induce behaviours.

The individual has always had to struggle to keep from being overwhelmed by the tribe. If you try it, you will be lonely often, and sometimes frightened. But no price is too high to pay for the privilege of owning yourself.

Friedrich Nietzsche

Life will break you.
Regardless.
So love deeply
Regardless.
And when hurt, remember.
And surrender to joy.

So what does it mean to be honest with yourself? Self-honesty is all about owning the present moment.

1. In which life situations am I not satisfied?
2. Why do I feel this way?
3. What would I wish these situations to be instead?
4. When do I feel my best?
5. Why do I not have more of these moments when life flows as I wish?
6. What is stopping me from achieving my dreams?
7. In which situations and with who do I feel powerless?
8. What would be my top 10 lists of dreams if I could do anything?
9. What do I believe about myself?
10. How do I honestly feel in my body?
11. What am I good at and don't give myself enough credit for?
12. Where do I overvalue myself and pretend to be better than I am?

In marriage
you are not sacrificing
yourself to the other
person.
You are sacrificing
yourself to the
relationship.

Joseph Campbell

When a person can't find a deep sense of meaning, they distract themselves with pleasure.

Victor Frankel

Someone I loved once gave me a box full of Darkness. It took me years to understand that this too was a gift.

Mary Oliver

After venting to someone, do you ever just sit back and think, I should've kept that to myself.

I used to think that my side of the story needed to be told to keep the facts right. Now I don't care what you choose to believe.

I have love in me the likes of which you can scarcely imagine and rage the likes of which you would not believe. If I cannot satisfy one, I will indulge the other.

Mary Shelley

When you are a child, you want to be a teenager. When you are a teenager you want to be an adult. When you are an adult you want to be a cat.

Girl, look at you. Everything that's happened in your life, you've fucking handled. You work hard, you are strong, you are ambitious, you are resilient. You are genuine and loyal. Anyone who doesn't value what you bring to the table, doesn't deserve you. You are a Queen.

You own everything that happened to you. Tell your stories. If people wanted you to write warmly about them, they should have behaved better.

@annelamott

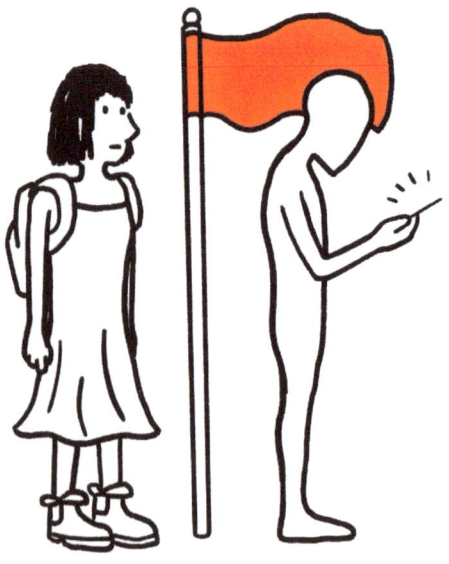

Most relationships don't end because couples stop loving each other, they end because one of the two stopped giving the other attention, communication, security and affirmation they need.

MY FRIENDSHIP CIRCLE OVER THE PAST FEW YEARS:

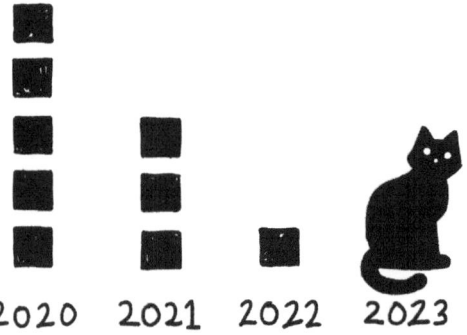

Don't let anyone tell you that you can't turn your toxic relationship into a healthy one. If you are with someone worth fighting for, separate and re-discover the reasons you fell in love. Promise that if you both give 150%, you will come back together stronger than ever.

This Time You Save Yourself.
You have spent too much time
Justifying their actions
To the jury in your mind
That knows you deserve better

If you find yourself unable to delve into deeper waters with another person, remember this. Intimacy is cultivated through moments of vulnerability, of allowing yourself to let your guard down and feel everything that needs to be felt, fully and completely. Not everyone is willing to traverse those murky waters with you or even without you. People can only meet you as far as they've met themselves, so remember that the next time you start to take on the pain of another's inability to face themselves and all that comes with that.

You cannot go much further when the fear of feeling trumps the hope of healing.

Unpopular fact: How he treats you, is how he feels about you. Don't try to decode it or make excuses. It's simple. If he acts like he doesn't care, he doesn't care, because if he truly liked you, he wouldn't put you in a position where you had to wonder why he acts the way he does, but claims he loves you. He'd just act right, and show you what you're truly worth.

Death may be the greatest of all human blessings.

Socrates

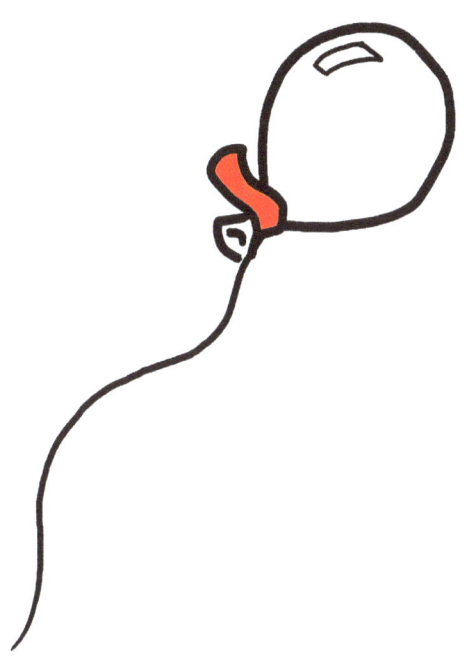

Can we start celebrating break ups? I just think finally realizing you deserve more than your partner is willing to give you, even if that means being alone, deserves cake and balloons. I really do.

Lane Moore @hellolanemoore

In the end, they both lost ... He lost a woman that would've never given up on him and she lost the woman she was before he broke her heart.

I wasn't sure what to make for dinner, so I opened a bottle of wine and now I don't care.

Between stimulus and response there is a space. In that space is our power to choose our response. In our response lies our growth and our freedom.

Victor Frankel

My therapist once told me that someone who's emotionally unavailable can often make someone who's emotionally available feel like their basic needs are too much.

Stop holding on to who he was supposed to be.
He lied.

@mamaguidetodivorce

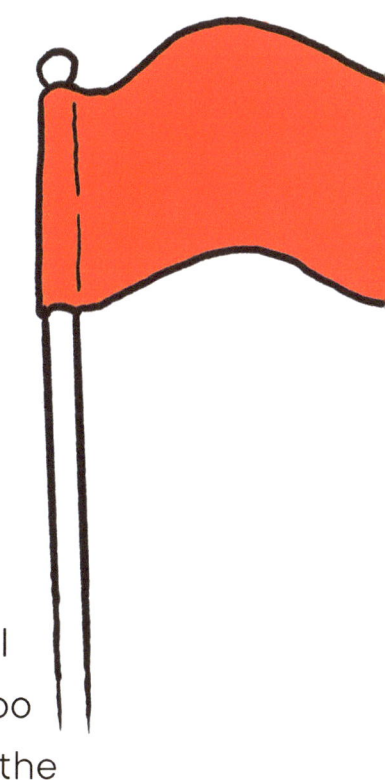

Finally I realised that I was never asking for too much. I was just asking the wrong person.

Healing wasn't rosemary baths and candles and tea;
It was ugly crying in the shower.

@l.e.bowman

She doesn't know how to feel right now. One minute she feels like she's healing, the next minute she's questioning her self-worth. One minute she's laughing and smiling, the next she's crying while desperately trying to keep it together. Hoping one day it'll all make sense.

@rl_saul

I thought
you were
my person,
but instead
you were my most painful lesson.
And I'm still trying
to come to terms with
how two people
can seemingly
have it all
one moment
and the next
be nothing more
than strangers.

I don't know what it is like to not have deep emotions. Even when I feel nothing, I feel it completely.

Sylvia Plath

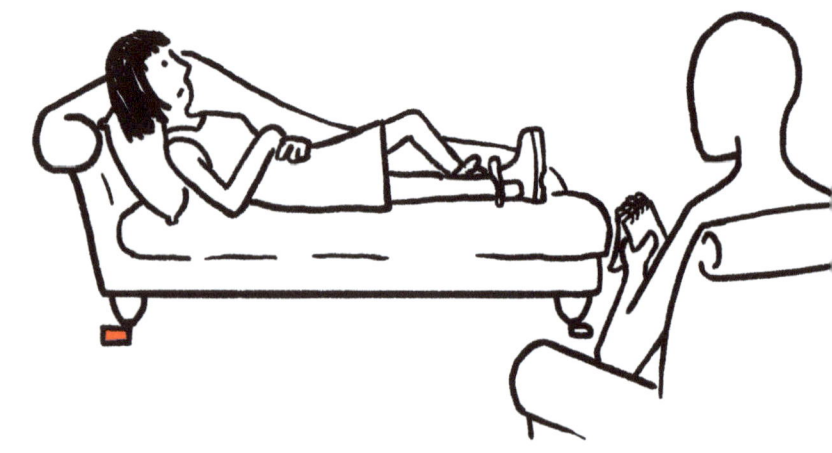

Your thoughts lie.

my therapist

Men don't have to be perfect to make women happy.

All a man really needs to do is love her like he promised when they first dated.

Even the strongest feeling expires when ignored and taken for granted.

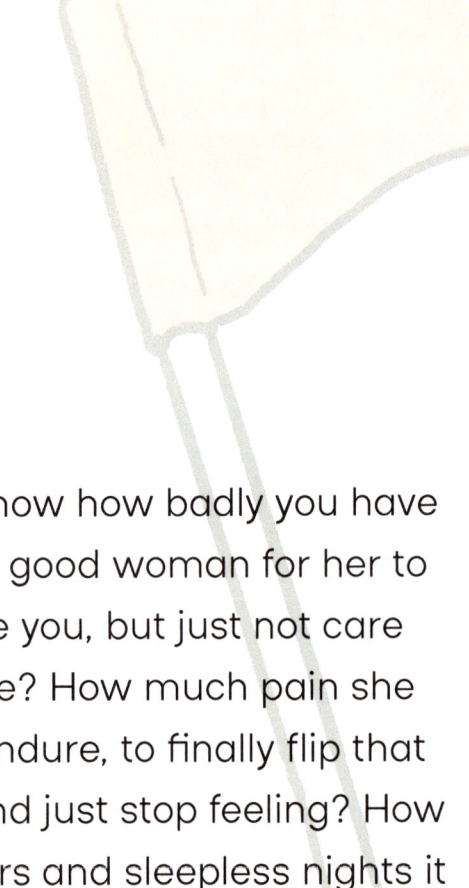

Do you know how badly you have to hurt a good woman for her to still love you, but just not care anymore? How much pain she had to endure, to finally flip that switch, and just stop feeling? How many tears and sleepless nights it took, before she finally gave up? Yeah ... I didn't think so.

@clspoetry

Quantum science suggests the existence of many possible futures for each moment of our lives.
Each future lies in a state of rest until it is awakened by choices made in the present.

@gregg.baden

And so I poured my own love
Into my own beautiful soul until
It was so full that it no longer
Settled for scraps.

*@kristinkory_*

If you catch yourself BEGGING someone for ... human decency? A response? Time together? Clarity? Respect? Some compassion? Some kindness?
You need to take a step back and realise that you're begging someone for the bare minimum. That's ridiculous and beneath you. Fuck that.

Erich Dust

Don't love too deeply
Until you're sure that the other person
Loves you with the same depth
Because the depth of your love today is
The depth of your wound tomorrow.

Nizar Qabbani

May the tears we cried in 2023 water the seeds we are planting in 2024

@playlist

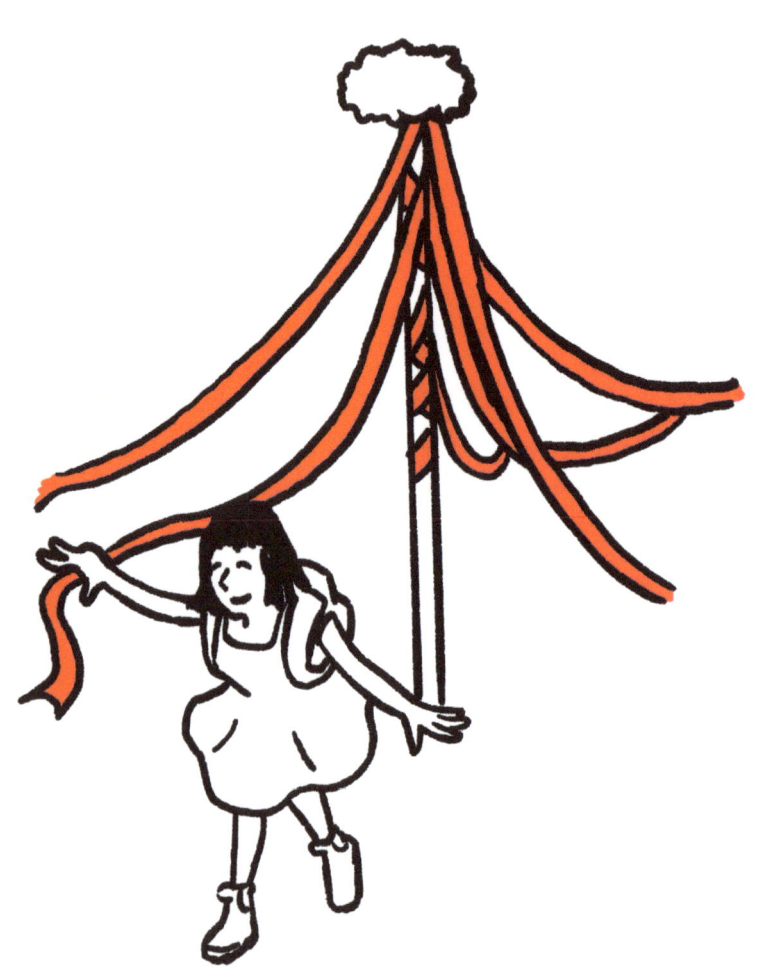

Be happy on purpose. Go outside. Stretch. Read a book. Call a friend. Meditate. Write in a journal. Drink water. Eat good food. Breathe. Learn something new. Express gratitude. Chase the sun. Dance. Create magic.

You are perfect exactly
as you are.
There is no need to
change anything except the
thoughts that you are not
good enough.

@naturallife

Acknowledgements

A big thank you to emerging artist Thomas Corboy for accepting the challenge to illustrate my interpretations of the quotes and red flags. His skillful, quirky and deft illustrations beautifully capture the essence of the text.

A ginormous thank you to friends who (perhaps unwittingly) became my survival team providing love, care and space: Danny, Jane, James, Kirsty, Margi, Chris, Joanne, Linda, Evelyn and Lyn.

Thanks to Jane Ormond and Dominique Bongiovanni for editing and design advice.

And big hugs to Daphne Dot who gifted laughter through the darkness when I thought it would never return.

Lessons learned:

- Thoughts lie
- One's comfort zone is a place of deceit
- Alone comes in different flavors
  – aloneness, lonely, loneliness
- Medication offers time-out to practice survival strategies

References

All quotes, poems and comments were sourced from Instagram. While many were anonymous, known authors or publishers were contacted for permission to include. IG handles are provided so you can follow these talented wordsmiths.

The Uses of Sorrow by Mary Oliver, reprinted by the permission of The Charlotte Sheedy Literary Agency as agent for the author. Copyright © 2006 by Mary Oliver with permission of Bill Reichblum

The Divine Matrix: Bridging Time, Space, Miracles, and Belief by Gregg Braden, Hay House, 2008. http://www.greggbraden.com @gregg.braden

What I Learned from the Trees by Lauren E Bowman, reprinted with permission by Button Poetry 2021 https://buttonpoetry.com/l-e-bowman @l.e.bowman

A Medicine Woman's Prayer by Sheree Bliss Tilsley reprinted with permission by Sheree Bliss Tilsley www.shereeblisstilsley.com @shereeblisstilsley

@mamaguidetodivorce

@NaturalLife

@rl_saul

@someecards

Anne Lamott

Christie L Starkweather @clspoetry

Dr Vassilia @JunoCounselling https://www.junocounseling.com

Friedrich Nietzsche

Gregg Braden

Jamie Anderson

Joseph Campbell

L.E. Bowman, Learned from the Trees, Button Poetry

Lane Moore @hellolanemoore

Marianne Williamson

Mary Oliver

Mary Shelley

Nizar Qabbani

Sheree Bliss Tilsley – Falcon Spirit Healing

Socrates

Sylvia Plath

Thich Nhat Hanh

Victor Frankel

Books by the Author

Available via Amazon and other online bookstores

Dancing the Labyrinth

The Bringer of Happiness

Delphi

www.kazjoypress.com

www.ingramcontent.com/pod-product-compliance
Lightning Source LLC
Chambersburg PA
CBHW042350300426
44109CB00035B/143